S. LUCIA KANTER ST. AMOUR

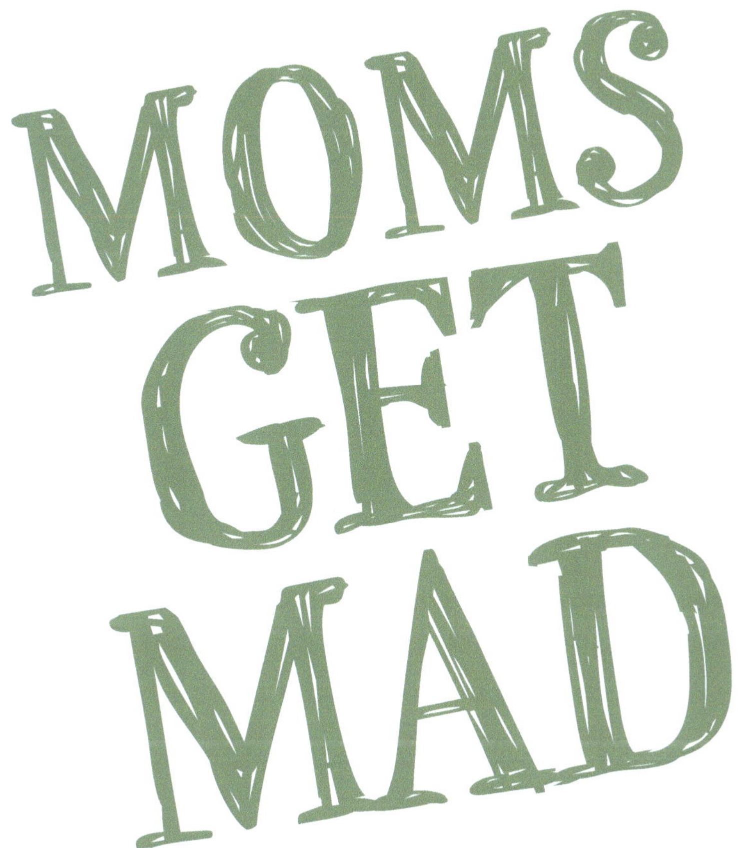

Copyright 2007, 2024 Pactum Factum Press

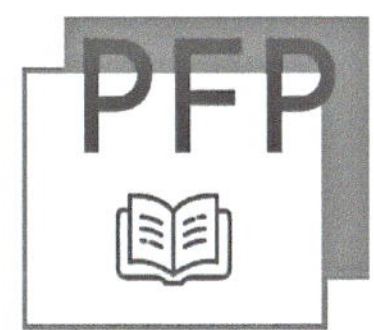

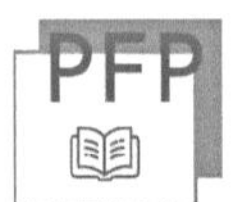 Copyright © 2024 Pactum Factum Press,
447 Sutter St, Ste 405, San Francisco, CA 94108

2023 Library of Congress Copyright Registration #: TXu 2-352-677

Printed in the United States.

Book design by Asya Blue Design.

ISBN: 979-8-9864461-7-2 Hardcover
ISBN: 979-8-9864461-8-9 Paperback

For the two luminous souls who, once upon a time, were my favorite reason to lose sleep, cry, and sing "Dancing Queen."

You know who you are.

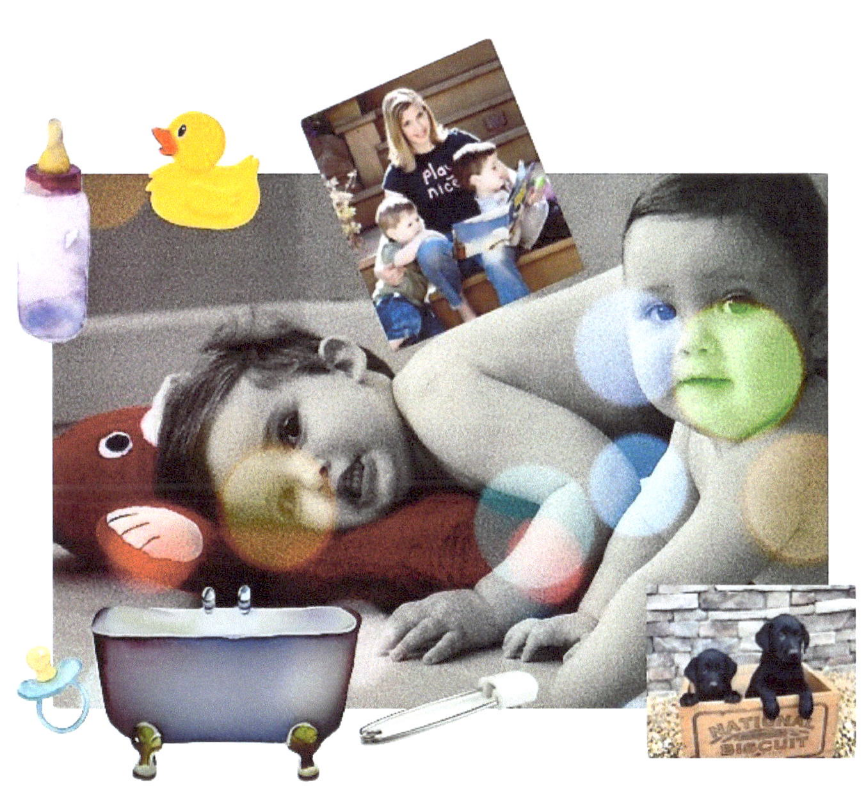

Good morning, good day! You mustn't delay

It's five in the morning and baby wails

"HEY!"

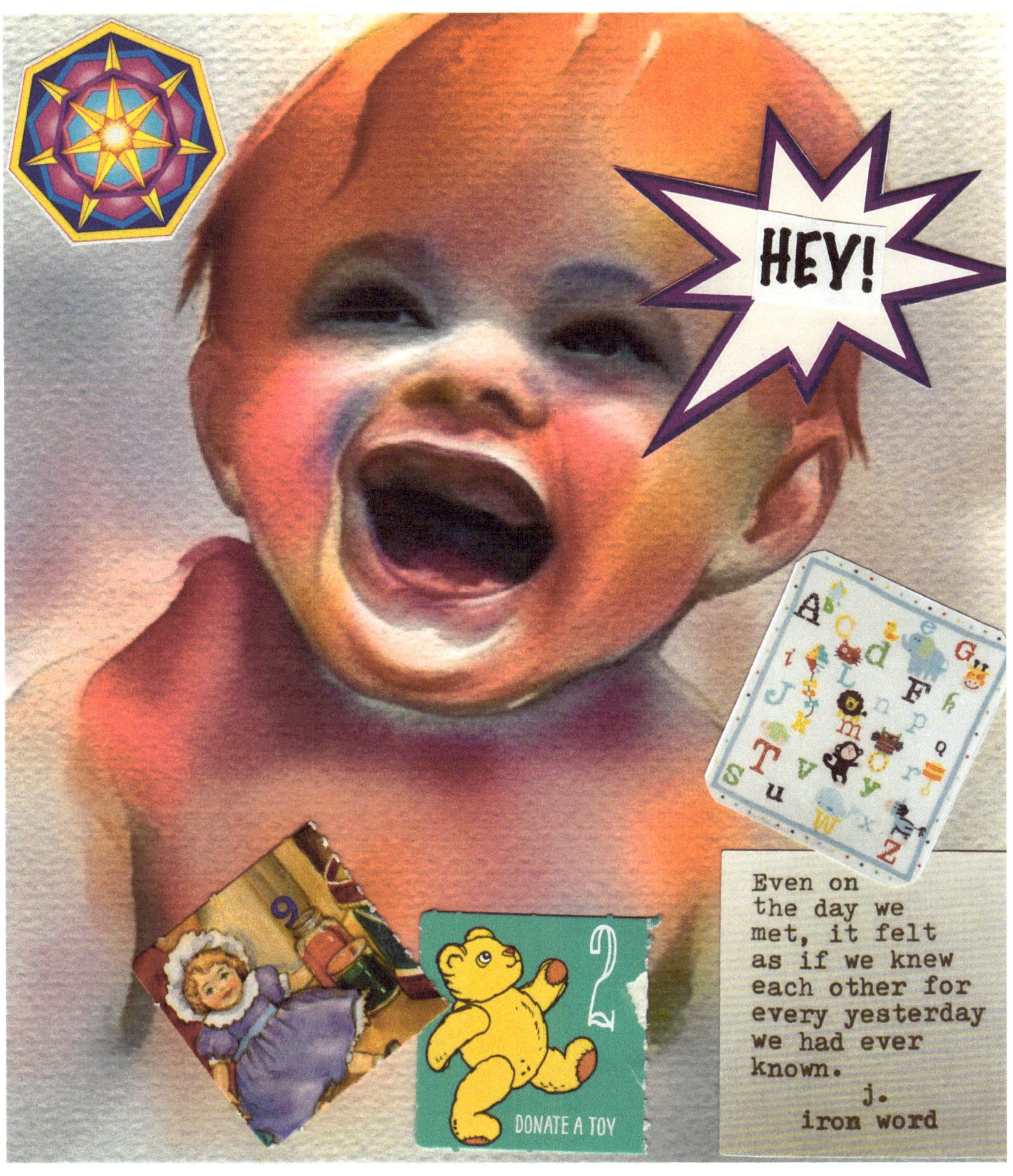
HEY!
DONATE A TOY
Even on
the day we
met, it felt
as if we knew
each other for
every yesterday
we had ever
known.
        j.
    iron word

Coo to me, bounce with me, feed me right now!

The need is so urgent, I just can't say how

—

'Cause shrieking's my way of telling you so

That's how I'm made, you can't blame me you know

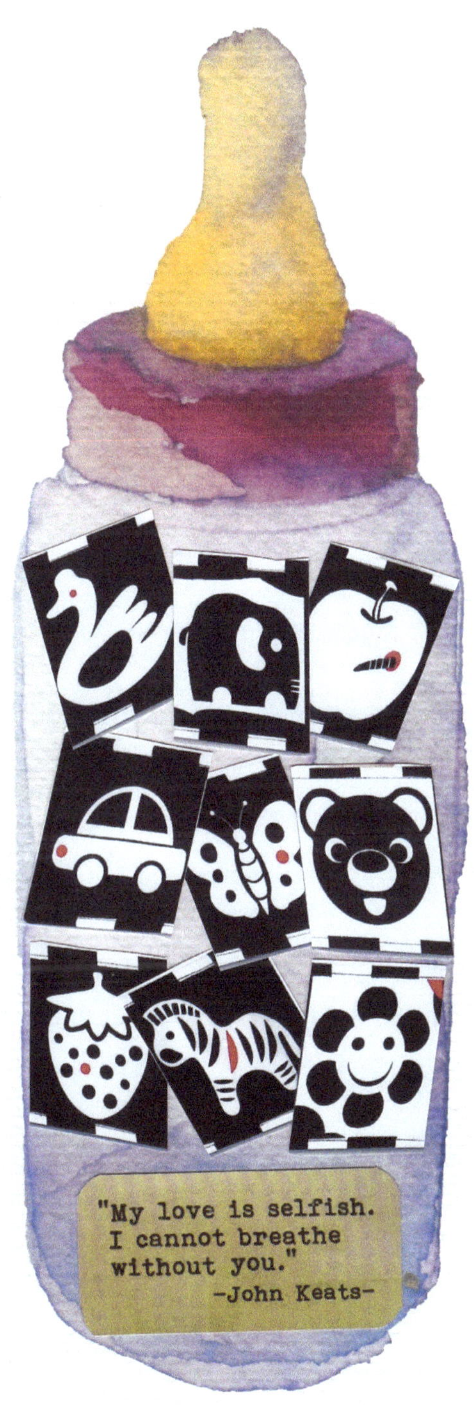
"My love is selfish.
I cannot breathe
without you."
-John Keats-

Mom can't eat and can't sleep, she can't pee on the potty

Can't talk on the phone or even do laundry

———

"Oh please, what's the big deal?" you may ask of her disarray

"It seems pretty sweet to hang out and stroll all day"

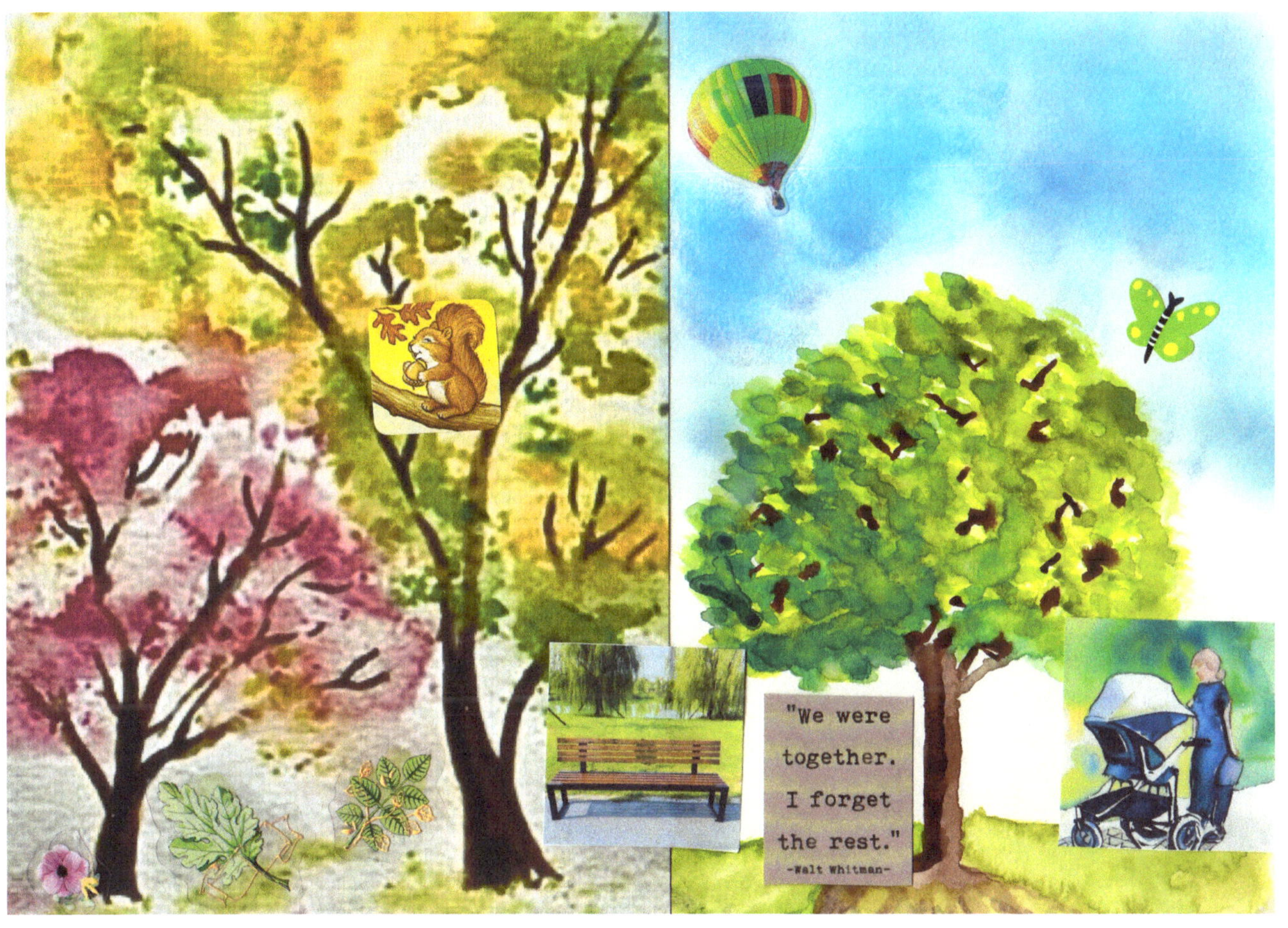

"We were
together.
I forget
the rest."
-Walt Whitman-

Well, she's wiping and chasing and reading the Experts

With advice from all sides and, by the way, who asked her?

—

They tell her to nourish and raise you just right

They'd be your perfect Mommy, except for not being
there in the middle of the night

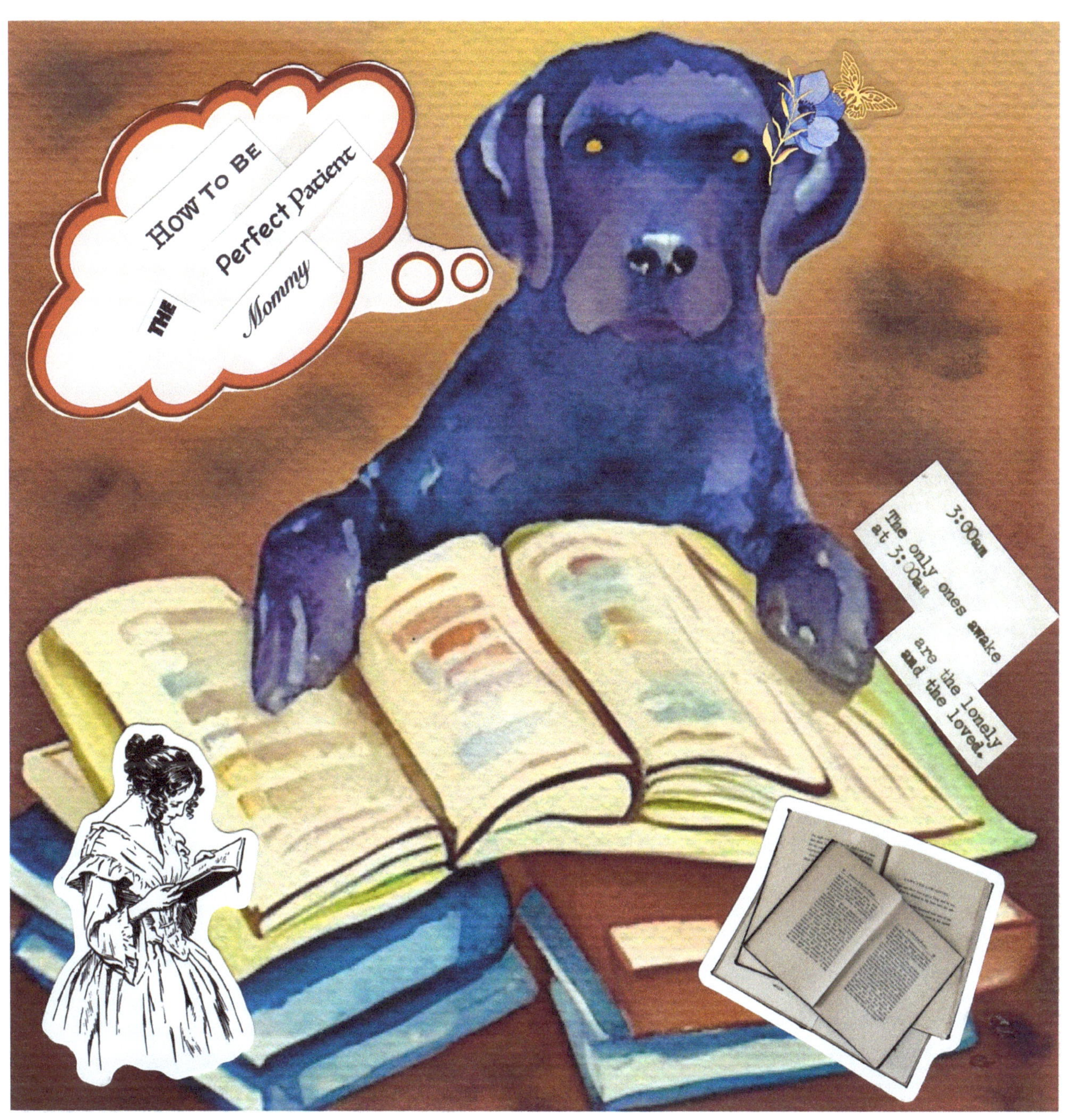
How To Be
THE
Perfect Patient
Mommy
3:00am
The only ones awake
at 3:00am
are the lonely
and the loved.

And since when was Mom a contortionist

In a job that's ergonomically unfit?

———

A wry joke is the curious biological flaw

That just when she needs a third arm, evolution withdraws

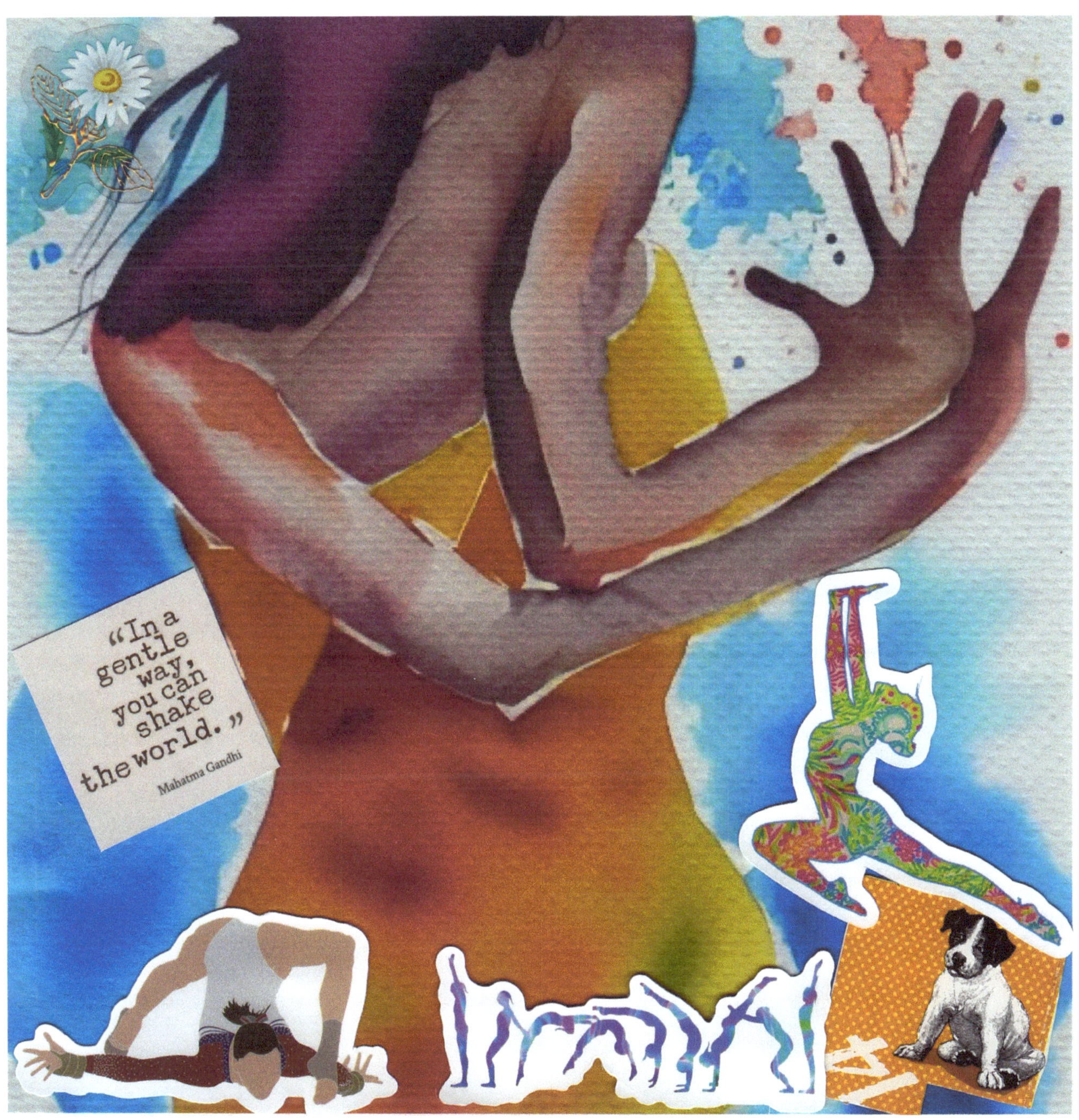
"In a gentle way, you can shake the world."
Mahatma Gandhi

Despite all the noise, Mom tries hard so you're happy

And just when she thinks she can breathe:
pee-yew, another stinky nappy!

———

She would change you that instant so you'd smell like a winner

If only your toddling brother wasn't about to sip paint thinner

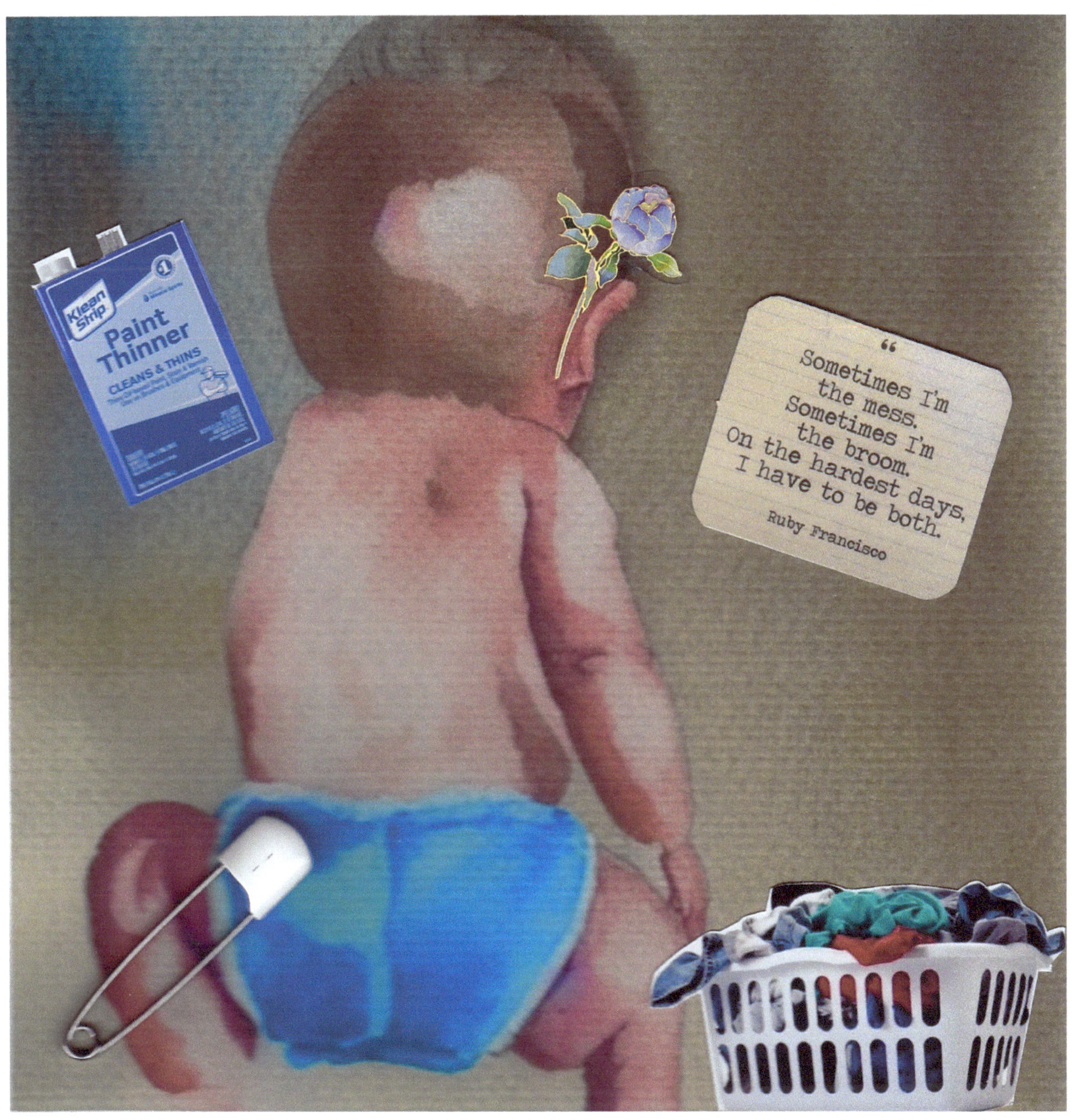
Klean Strip
Paint
Thinner
CLEANS & THINS

"
Sometimes I'm
the mess.
Sometimes I'm
the broom.
On the hardest days,
I have to be both.

Ruby Francisco

When she finds a rare nano-moment to think,

She notices her previous life is extinct

———

She used to play tennis, learn Chopin and French

To converse wittily … {sigh} skills now sidelined on the bench

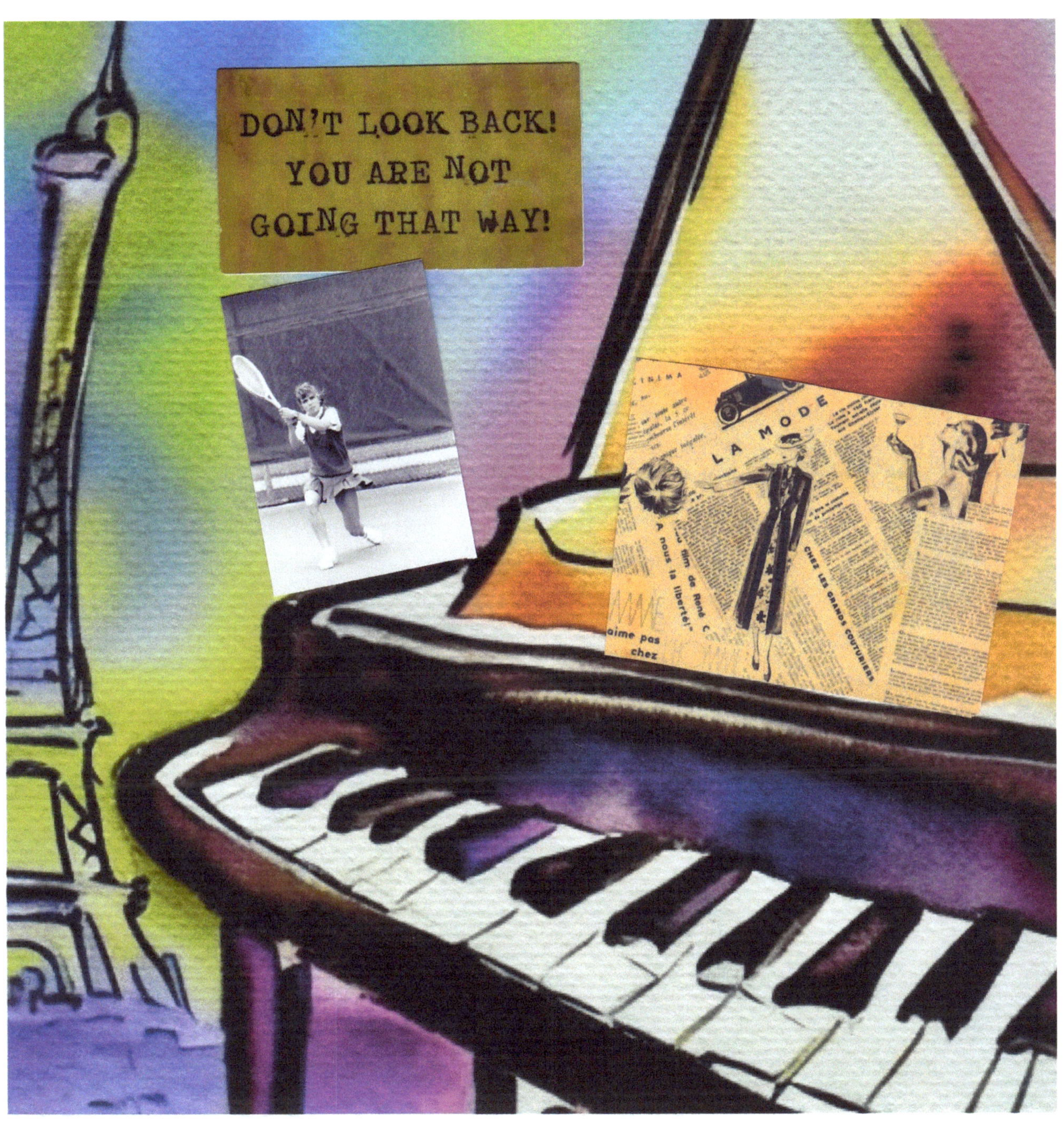
DON'T LOOK BACK!
YOU ARE NOT
GOING THAT WAY!
LA MODE

Back then, she didn't know how it felt

To get giddy for garbage trucks, or watch ice cream melt

—

She didn't gaze awestruck at airplanes or frogs

Now, her grooming standards have devolved from: "Is it clean?"
to "Well, as long as it doesn't smell like the dog …"

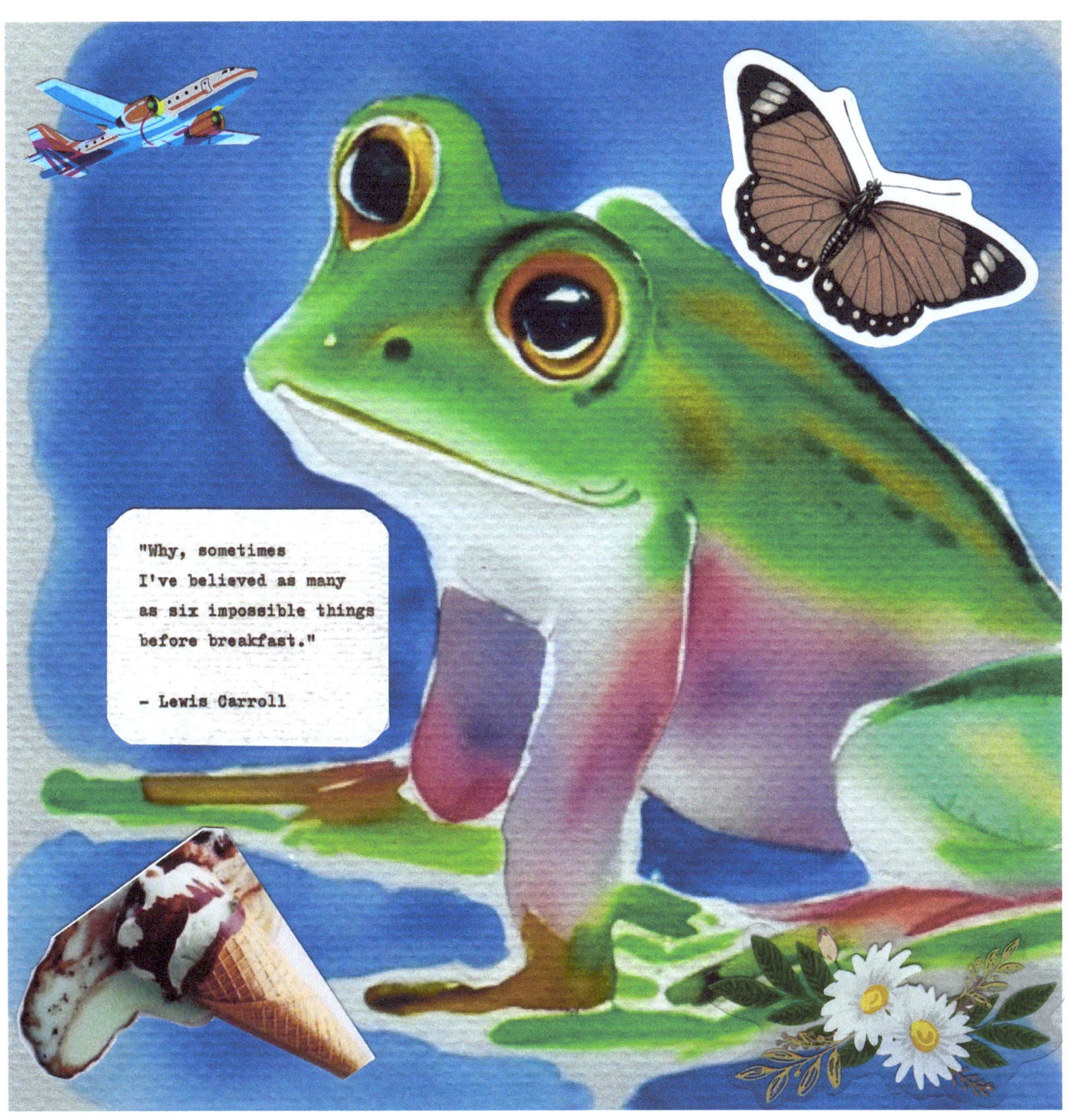
"Why, sometimes
I've believed as many
as six impossible things
before breakfast."

- Lewis Carroll

By five in the evening, Mom's patience is spent

She {ugh} loses her cool – at who? A cutie who
doesn't even pay rent

The last thing to do when mom is so beat, is to inquire
"What's wrong with you -- can't take the heat?"

She just needs a rest, she just needs a break; it's not
too much to ask, or to take

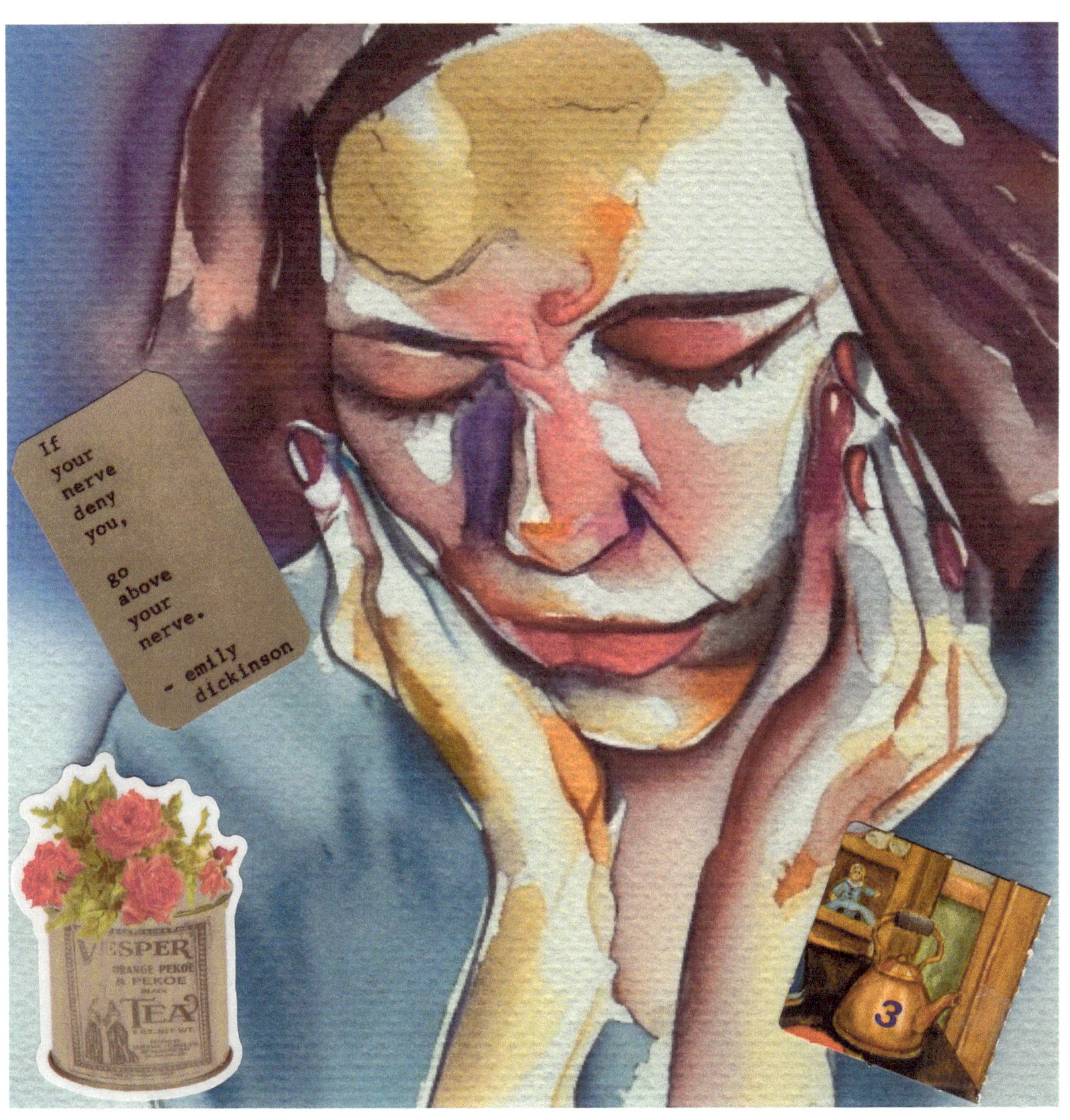
If
your
nerve
deny
you,

go
above
your
nerve.

- emily
dickinson

VESPER
ORANGE PEKOE
& PEKOE
TEA

3

Instead try to wait while Mom counts to ten

Or sings "Dancing Queen" or confides in a friend

—

It doesn't take much to quiet her bark:

A nuzzle, a grin, a silly drawing of Uncle Mark

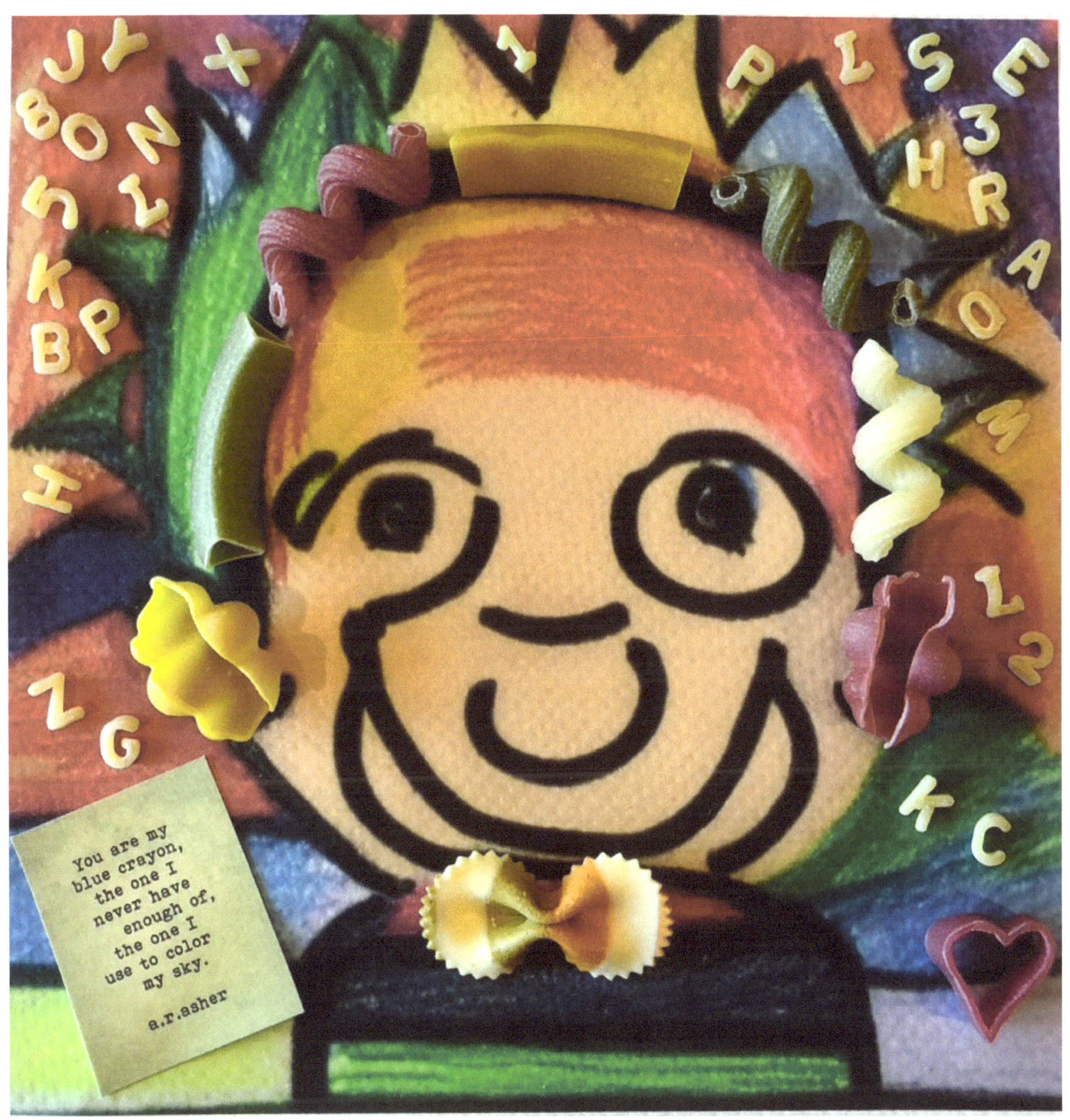
You are my
blue crayon,
the one I
never have
enough of,
the one I
use to color
my sky.

a.r.asher

It may be as simple as hearing you laugh

(And you know what wouldn't hurt? A nice long bubble bath)

———

Don't worry, don't fret - Moms get mad, after all

She's not crazy or cruel - just runs out of charge, that's all

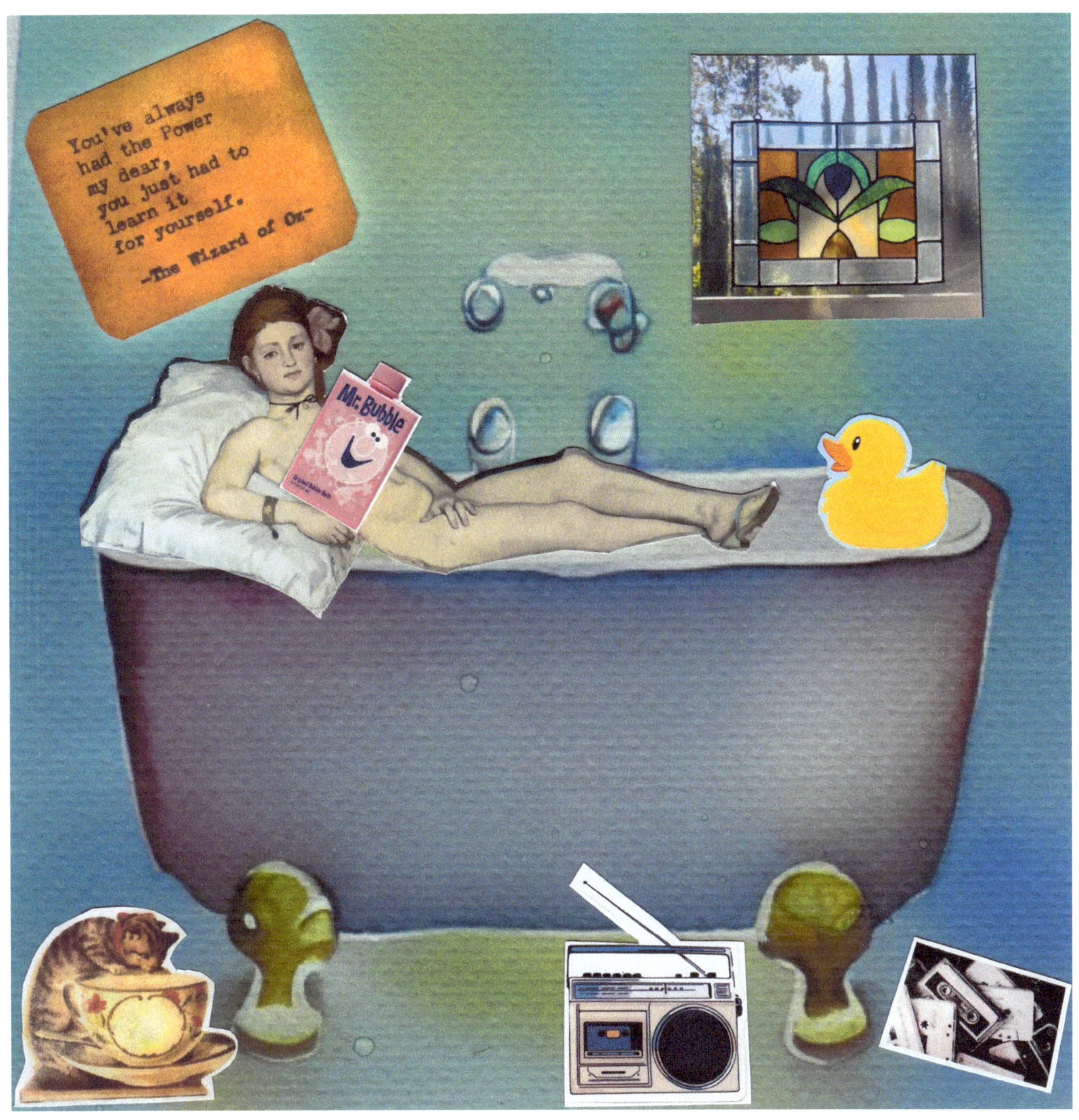
You've always
had the Power
my dear,
you just had to
learn it
for yourself.

—The Wizard of Oz—

Mr. Bubble

It's not your job to ease her distress

Truly – the situation is not such a mess

Right now go to sleep – really, I mean it

'Cause tomorrow she'll tickle you 'til you can't stand it!

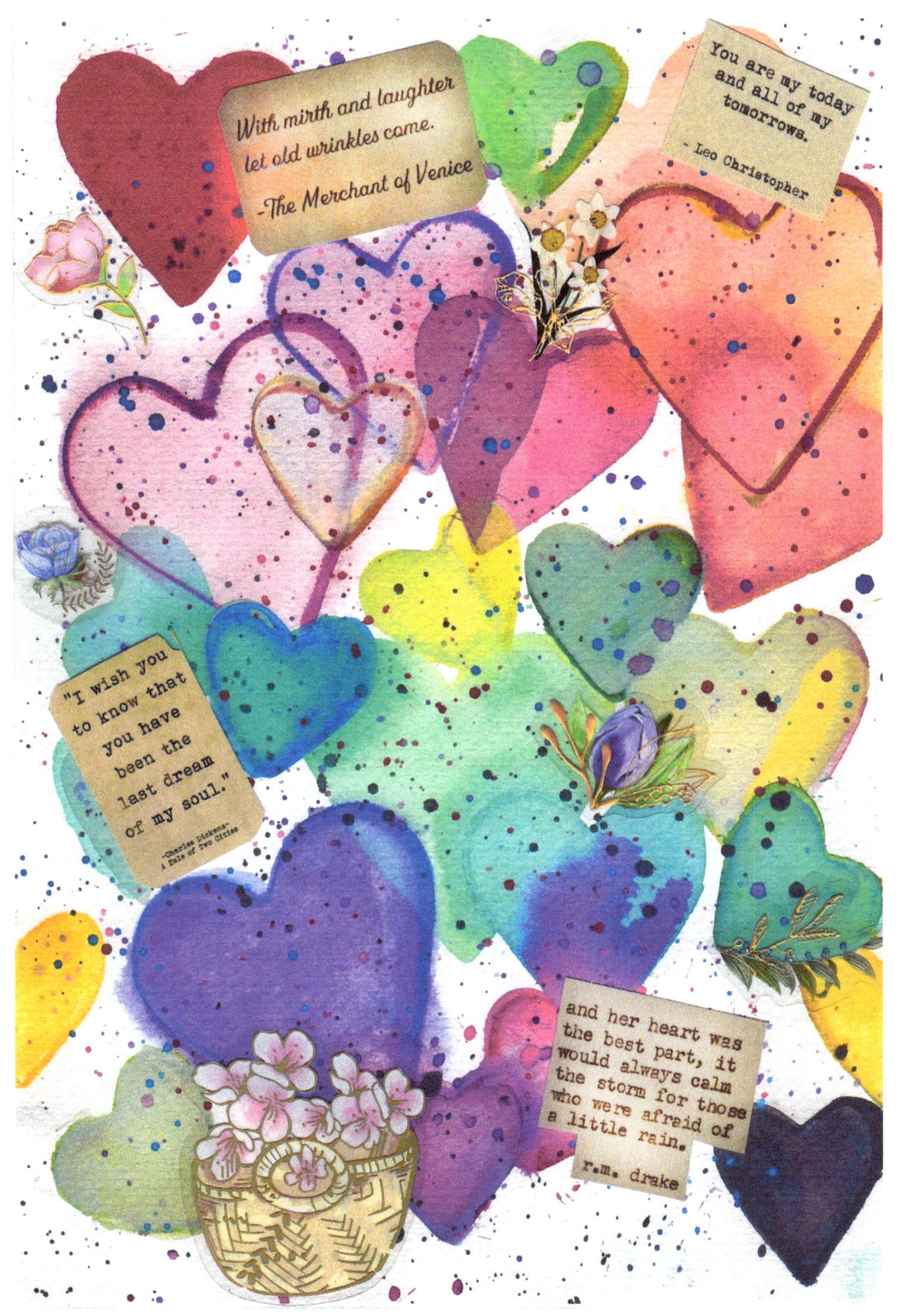
With mirth and laughter
let old wrinkles come.

-The Merchant of Venice

You are my today
and all of my
tomorrows.

~ Leo Christopher

"I wish you
to know that
you have
been the
last dream
of my soul."

-Charles Dickens-
A Tale of Two Cities

and her heart was
the best part, it
would always calm
the storm for those
who were afreid of
a little rain.

r.m. drake

About the Author

Lucia is an attorney action figure; unapologetic amateur artist; and restless writer of books, articles and essays. A special needs parent and mom of 5 boys (3 canine & 2 human), she feels all the feels.

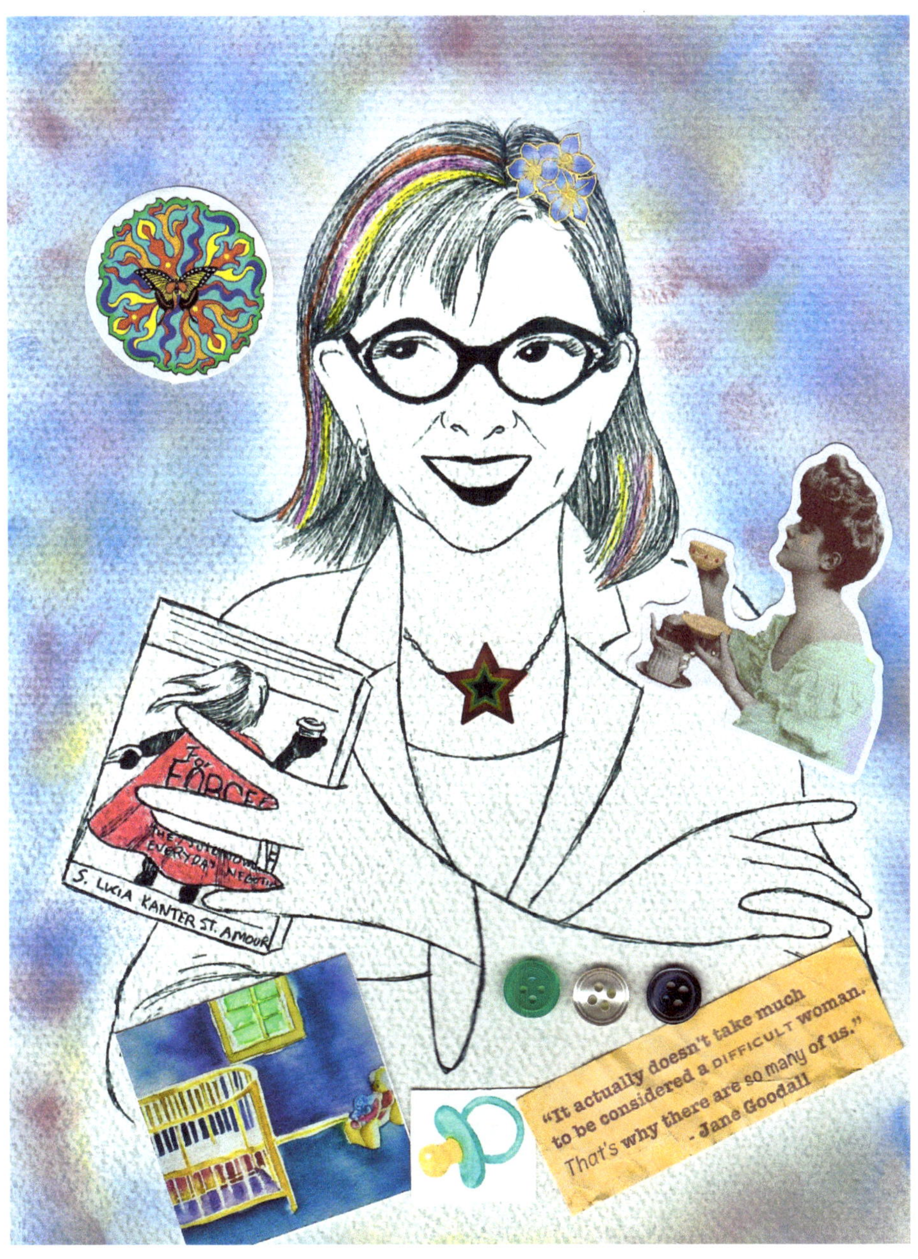

About the Art

As a parent, and especially a special needs parent, one accumulates quite the collection of arts & crafts accoutrements over the years. After 19 years, the project cupboard is brimming with crayons, stickers, pipe cleaners, popsicle sticks, watercolor tubes, watercolor brush paints, watercolor pencils, regular colored pencils, sharpie markers in a dozen colors, pastels, acrylics, assorted distressed ink pads, various forms of adhesive, multiple cutting tools and punches, sundry papers (construction, photo, faux textured, watercolor, magazines). Not to mention prosaic household items such as pasta (even miniature alphabet pastina), buttons, diaper pins, cookie cutters—even the numbered doors from years of cardboard chocolate advent calendars at Christmas time (just ... autism ... it's hard to explain). Sure, collage and other art can all be accomplished digitally and by A.I. these days (no tiny scraps of trimmed paper to tidy, no spilled glitter on the dog). But this list of sensory satisfying supplies contributed to the jaunty, nonsensical messes anointing these pages, created by the whirring mind and bustling hands of the author:

Cover art licensed by the author from Shutterstock and modified by Asya Blue Design